BUSINESS
JAPAN

BUSINESS JAPAN

A Practical Guide to Understanding Japanese Business Culture

Peggy Kenna   **Sondra Lacy**

Printed on recyclable paper

PASSPORT BOOKS
a division of *NTC Publishing Group*
Lincolnwood, Illinois USA

Library of Congress Cataloging-in-Publication Data

Kenna, Peggy.
   Business Japan: a practical guide to understanding Japanese business
culture / Peggy Kenna, Sondra Lacy.
     p. cm.
   ISBN 0-8442-3552-0
   1. Business etiquette—Japan.   2. Corporate culture—Japan.
   3. Business communication—Japan.   4. Negotiation in business—
Japan.   I. Lacy, Sondra.   II. Title.
HF389.K455   1994
395'.52'0952—dc20   93—42809
                                   CIP

Published by Passport Books, a division of NTC Publishing Group.
4255 West Touhy Avenue, Lincolnwood, (Chicago) Illinois 60646-1975, U.S.A.
©1994 by NTC Publishing Group. All rights reserved.
No part of this work may be reproduced, stored in a retrieval system
or transmitted in any form or by any means,
electronic or mechanical, including photocopying and recording or otherwise
without the prior permission of NTC Publishing Group.
Manufactured in the United States of America.

4 5 6 7 8 9 0 VP 9 8 7 6 5 4 3 2 1

Contents

Peggy Kenna is a communication specialist working with foreign-born professionals in the American workplace. She provides cross-cultural training and consultation services to companies who are conducting business internationally. She is also a certified speech and language pathologist who specializes in accent modification. Peggy lives in Tempe, Arizona.

Sondra Lacy is a certified communication specialist who teaches American communication skills to foreign-born professionals in the American workplace. She also provides cross-cultural training and consultation services to companies conducting business internationally. Sondra lives in Scottsdale, Arizona.

Business Japan is an invaluable tool for thousands of entrepreneurs, businesspeople, corporate executives, technicians, and salespeople seeking to develop lasting business relationships in Japan.

The book provides a fast, easy way for you to become acquainted with business practices and protocol to help you increase your chances for success in Japan. You will discover the secrets of doing business internationally while improving your interpersonal communication skills.

Let this book work for you.

> Pam Del Duca
> President/CEO
> The DELSTAR Group
> Scottsdale, Arizona

 Entrepreneur Of The Year®
Award Recipient

Welcome to Business Japan

Business Japan offers a smooth and problem-free transition between the American and Japanese business cultures.

This pocket-size book contains information you need when traveling in Japan or doing business with Japanese colleagues. It explains the differences in business culture you will encounter in such areas as:

- Business etiquette

- Communication style

- Problem solving and decision making

- Meetings and presentation style

Business Japan gets you started on the right tracks and challenges you to seek ways to improve your success in the global marketplace by understanding cultural differences in the ways people communicate and do business with each other.

Successful international companies are able to adapt to the business styles acceptable in other countries and by other nationalities, based on their knowledge and awareness of key cultural differences. These differences, if not acknowledged and addressed, can interfere in successful communication and can adversely affect the success of any business attempting to expand internationally.

Business Japan is designed to overcome such difficulties by comparing the American culture with the culture of Japan. Identifying appropriate behavior in one's own culture can make it easier to adapt to that of the country with which you are doing business. With this in mind, the book's unique parallel layout allows an at-a-glance comparison of Japanese business practices with those of the United States.

Practical and easy to use, *Business Japan* will help you win the confidence of Japanese associates and achieve common business goals.

The global environment today is a multicultural one. While general business considerations are essentially the same the world over, business styles differ greatly from country to country. What is customary and appropriate in one country may be considered unusual or even offensive in another. The increasingly competitive environment calls for an individual approach to each national market. The success of your venture outside your home market depends largely upon preparation. The American style of business is not universally accepted. Yet we send our employees, executives, salespeople, technicians to negotiate or carry out contracts with little or no understanding of the cultural differences in the ways people communicate and do business with each other. How many business deals have been lost because of this cultural myopia?

Globalization is a process which is drawing people together from all nations of the world into a single community linked by the vast network of communication technologies. Technological breakthroughs in the past two decades have made instant communication between individuals around the world an affordable reality.

As these technological advances continue to open up and expand the dialogue among members of the world community, the need for effective communication between nations and peoples has accelerated.

When change occurs as dramatically and rapidly as we have witnessed in the past decade, many people throughout the world are being forced to quickly learn and adapt to unfamiliar ways of doing things. Some actually welcome change and the opportunities it presents, while others are reluctant to give up familiar ways of doing things. History proves that cultures are slow to change. But, individuals who are mentally prepared to accept change and deal with differences can successfully understand and adapt to cultures very different from their own.

A culture develops when individuals have common experiences and share their reactions to these experiences by communicating with other members of their society.

Over time, communication becomes the vehicle by which cultural beliefs and values are developed, shared and transmitted from one generation to the next. Communication and culture are mutually dependent.

Effective communication between governments or international businesses requires more than being able to speak the language fluently or relying on expert interpreters. Understanding the language is only the first step. Understanding and accepting the behaviors, customs and attitudes of other cultures is also required to bring harmony and success in the worldwide business and political arena.

The importance of the influence of one's native culture on the way one approaches life cannot be overstated. Each country's cultural beliefs and values are reflected in its people's idea of the "right" way to live and behave.

In general, businesspeople who practice low-key, non-adversarial, win/win techniques in doing business abroad tend to be most successful. Knowing what your company wants to achieve, its bottom line, and also understanding the objectives of the other party and helping to accommodate them in the business transaction are necessary for developing long-term, international business relationships.

Often, representatives from American companies, for example, have difficulty doing business with *each other*, even when they speak the same language and share a common culture. Consider how much more difficult it is to do business with people from different cultures who speak different languages.

Success in the international business arena will not be easy for those who do not take steps to gain the skills necessary to be global players. The language barrier is an obvious problem.

Equally important will be negotiation skills, as well as an understanding of and adaptation to the social and business etiquette of the foreign country. Americans have a reputation for failing to appreciate this. In other words, businesspeople doing business abroad will get off to a good start if they remember to do the following:

- Listen closely; understand both verbal and non-verbal communication.

- Focus on mutual interests, not differences.

- Nurture long-term relationships.

- Emphasize quality. Be prepared to defend the quality of your products and services, and the quality of your business relationship.

Understanding Japanese Culture

Japan is the most industrialized nation in the Pacific Rim and one of the foremost traders in the global marketplace. Since World War II, Japan has had great economic success. This has been attributed to an intelligent and diligent workforce, trade barriers that keep out imports, and allocation of less than 1% of the GNP for defense.

Japan is one of the most difficult markets to penetrate, but it can be a profitable one. Japan heavily imports food products and raw materials as well as other industrial and high tech products.

Without a third party introduction, it is difficult to do business in Japan. This third party should be of appropriate rank such as a representative of a bank, large trading company or member of an acknowledged trade association. This third party can act as an intermediary during negotiations. In Japan, banks and trading companies can join the business ventures they support. You also need a local agent or distributor to sell your goods in Japan. Most importing and exporting is done through trading companies.

To many Westerners Japanese ways of thought and behavior are ambiguous, uncertain, and relative.

Westerners have to learn to interpret hints and subtleties and work with a greater degree of indirection and lack of clarity than they are used to. Westerners and Japanese do not share the same set of communication conventions. The meanings of body language, silence, manners, as well as language can get lost in translation.

To do business in Japan have patience. It may take two or three years to penetrate their market. Invest in the future. Be prepared to break down barriers between management and production people. If you are going to do business in Japan, most of your counterparts will want to know how your company can offer a better product or a better price than competitors.

Remember, that within each culture there are still many individual differences. There are also differences between companies; not all do business the same way. Also, remember that not all Pacific Rim countries have the same culture and communication style. There are some commonalities but each Pacific Rim country has a unique communication style and their business etiquette is subtly different.

United States

■ *Belief in competition*

Americans believe that competition is healthy and good and that it fosters creativity. Americans compete for achievement, for visibility, for the chance for promotion. However, Americans do not like outright conflict which they see as being inflexible and uncompromising.

■ *Relationships are short term*

To Americans, business relationships are not personal. They tend to trust the other party until proven wrong. Americans also tend to have little problem meeting strangers.

Americans believe that logic as well as communication skills is important; they believe that a rational appeal works best.

■ *Need for peace and harmony*

Japanese believe very strongly in avoiding confrontation and disagreement; they use compromise and conciliation. They also believe in collective responsibility for decisions as well as results.

The Japanese often will not tell their true feelings in order to maintain harmony.

■ *Building relationships important*

The Japanese system of doing business is intensely personal. Human relationships are seen as more important than logic. The Japanese believe it is very important to build a relationship of trust and this can take years to develop.

The Japanese like emotional appeals as well as logical/rational ones (facts and technical jargon).

The Japanese tend to feel uncomfortable with strangers. This is also true for other Pacific Rim countries in differing degrees.

United States

■ *Belief in equality*

Americans express a fundamental belief in the basic equality of all people. However, they often do not put this belief into practice.

A person's position in society is usually determined by his or her achievements and money is seen as a visible sign of this achievement. Ideally Americans try to minimize differences and find common ground. They also stress informality and spontaneity. They do not use titles much.

In American companies relationships can cross the boundaries of rank and seniority.

Japan

■ *Vertical society*

The Japanese do not have the same concept of equality as Americans. In fact, the reverse. Relationships in Japan are superior/subordinate. Employers are seen as parents; employees as children. Loyalty to superiors and to the company is considered a great virtue.

Japanese companies have an atmosphere of strict discipline in which rank and seniority are the foundation of all relationships. The Japanese need to determine your rank before they know how to relate to you. Business cards can provide this information. Give them out before performing greetings.

Communication Style

United States

■ *Admire fluency; dislike silence*

Americans are great talkers and tend to become uncomfortable with too much silence. Some also believe it's all right to brag and boast and occasionally exaggerate.

■ *Direct and to the point*

Americans prefer people to say what they mean. Because of this they tend to sometimes miss subtle nonverbal cues.

Americans are uncomfortable with ambiguousness; they don't like to have to "fill in the blanks."

■ *Sincerity*

To Americans it means free from pretense and deceit.

■ *Like silence*

The Japanese tend to be suspicious of words; they are more concerned with actions. They believe in using silence as a way of communicating. They also believe it is better to talk too little than too much.

■ *Indirect and ambiguous*

The Japanese tend to give very little explanation as to what they mean and their answers are often very vague.

The Japanese dislike saying no. They will not tell you if they don't understand. If they disagree or feel they can't do something, they will make a statement like "It is difficult." This usually means they don't feel they can do what you requested. They often leave sentences unfinished so the other person can conclude it in his or her own mind.

■ *Sincerity* ✳

To the Japanese sincerity means to properly discharge all of one's obligations in order that everything will flow smoothly and so harmony will be maintained.

United State

■ *Truth is absolute*

Americans believe that truth is absolute and not dependent on circumstances. A fact is either true or false and what is true for one person is true for everybody.

■ *Face saving less important*

To Americans accuracy is important but errors are tolerated. Admitting mistakes is seen as a sign of maturity. They believe you learn from failure and therefore encourage risk taking.

Americans believe criticism can and should be objective. However, all criticism should be done with tact.

■ *Truth is relative*

The Japanese believe truth is dependent upon circumstances and obligations to other people. Nothing should be allowed to disrupt the surface harmony of the individual, therefore the Japanese will often give an answer that they believe will please the listener.

Individual Japanese do not make judgments independently and therefore may not be able to tell what they know. Instead they may make up an answer.

■ *Face saving very important*

Accuracy is important to the Japanese and errors are not well accepted. A Japanese does not like being put in the position of having to admit a mistake or failure. This does not result in a lot of risk taking. They also are hesitant to admit they didn't understand something.

The Japanese also tend to see criticism as personal and don't understand how Americans can separate criticism of one's actions from criticizing someone personally.

Communication Style

United States

■ *Direct eye contact*

Direct eye contact is very important to Americans since they need to see the nonverbal cues the speaker is giving. Nonverbal cues are an important part of the American English language.

■ *"Yes" means agreement*

Americans look for clues such as nodding of the head or the listener saying "yes" or "uh huh" so they can determine if their arguments are succeeding.

■ *Avoid direct eye contact*

Holding the gaze of another person is considered rude. The Japanese generally focus on a person's neck or tie knot.

■ *"Yes" or nodding means "I hear"*

The Japanese do not judge information given to them so they do not indicate agreement or disagreement; they only nod to indicate they are listening. To the Japanese "yes" or nodding means they are listening to you.

United States

■ *Like to debate*

Americans believe in lively and forceful debate and that a good argument can bring out valid points and thus result in a better decision. They also believe that it is possible to disagree with someone but not attack them personally.

■ *Individual decision makers*

One person is usually given power to make the final decision and bear all responsibility. Decisions tend to go from the top down. However, decision makers are found at all levels depending on the importance of the decision. Lower levels often get a chance to provide input. Americans believe that those closest to a problem should have input in determining the solution.

■ *Status*

Power is more important than status and power is not always determined by title, maturity or education; it can be determined by force of personality and political savvy.

■ *Non argumentative*

The Japanese have difficulty debating because they do not separate issues from persons. To directly disagree is seen as rude. Japanese also tend to speak very softly.

■ *Group decision making*

The general manager is usually the one whose ultimate approval is needed for decisions. It is up to the manager to initiate the decision-making process, seek consensus and make recommendations. Top management participates primarily to approve and coordinate. All members of the company likely to be affected by the decision must approve it. This is very time consuming but there is no way to shortcut this process.

■ *Status*

Maturity (age) is essential. The Japanese believe that wisdom comes with maturity. A young man automatically stands lower on the status scale. Youth and personal power are not revered in Japan. An important title from a good, well-known company is impressive. Education is a status symbol, especially if obtained from a well-known institution.

United States

■ *Constant change*

Americans believe change is good but constant change causes established hierarchies and relationships to be repeatedly disrupted. The needs of the individual are subsidiary to the organization. Loyalty between employee and company is often temporary but expected to be wholehearted while it lasts.

■ *Independence*

Americans believe in teamwork rather than group consensus. Teams are both competitive and cooperative and there is communication between teams.

Americans believe individuals should be assertive and say what they think.

Each person has a well defined function in their company. Americans are uneasy with ambiguity and hidden hierarchies; they believe the organizational chart should basically reflect the power structure.

Information and/or orders flow down through the organizational chart until they reach the level at which they are carried out. Each person takes specific work orders from action plans which are decided upon in meetings.

■ *Strict and hierarchical*

The Japanese believe that one should never do anything above their status, that one should not infringe on anyone else's status and that one should not cut across hierarchical boundaries. The Japanese don't want repeated change and disruptions. Loyalty to the company is for a lifetime.

■ *Interdependence*

In Japanese companies there is much cohesion within each group but between groups there is much competition. Consensus within groups is necessary but can be difficult to achieve.

This results in interminable meetings, arduous decision making, sharing of blame as well as credit, keeping everyone in the group informed of everything, and open office plans.

Each group has specific rights and responsibilities and it is not advisable to try to get an individual Japanese to do something outside that person's ability.

The Japanese dislike direct, specific work orders but prefer being given general goals and direction.

United States

■ *Directive management*

In American companies someone is always in charge and there is a clear decision maker. Americans have little concept of shared responsibility. Whoever is put in charge of implementing a decision is expected to be completely accountable for its success or failure.

Americans are procedures oriented and like to outline exactly what is to be done. They believe that relationships only need to be established at the level of the decision maker.

■ *Planning is short term*

Planning in the U.S. tends to be short term even though Americans spend much time and effort planning concepts and establishing procedures to carry out the plan. Success or failure depends on the agreed upon plan. Planning is usually top down but can be bottom up. Good planning skills involve good interpersonal skills.

■ *Participative management*

No one person is in charge which can make it difficult to determine who makes the final decision. Relationships need to be established with each level of Japanese management.

The whole group is accountable for the success or failure of a decision since the whole group made the decision.

■ *Planning long term but flexible*

The Japanese are interested in long term planning and also tend to be good tactical planners. A plan, a contract, or the content of a transaction is very flexible to the Japanese. Personal relationships are more important to them than the details of a contract.

United States

■ *Aim for equality*

A subtle hierarchy is often observed in American companies which is determined by power, not seniority or status. However, people can move within the hierarchy. Americans believe that with hard work and determination anyone can be successful, which usually means earning a lot of money. They like to minimize differences by calling everyone by first name, not using titles and such. It can be difficult to know what rank someone has just by looking at the person and observing how others talk to him or her.

Americans value fairness and like to believe they treat people impartially and without favoritism.

■ *Public decision making*

Americans expect people to express their opinions openly, and in matters of public policy or group decision making the majority rules.

Japan

■ *Vertical society*

Japanese society has traditionally been hierarchical. The rules of status in Japan are important. Classes, groups, nobility and elite are meaningful concepts. The foreigners who through manner, education or accomplishments can present themselves as upper class receive more respect.

Since the foreigner has no designated position in the hierarchy, that person is often excluded from the decision-making process and is out of the information circle of a Japanese company.

■ *Private decision making*

The Japanese don't discuss, argue or express opinions openly at meetings. Decisions are made quietly and slowly by building consensus outside of meetings.

United States

■ *Linear time*

Westerners view time as a steady, straight progression. There is past, present and future; when a moment is gone, it is gone forever.

Americans tend to be very punctual. Business days are usually divided into segments to be completed. There is a beginning time and ending time for each part of a day. Therefore it is very important that each segment start on time or the whole day can be thrown off.

■ *Quick planning/implementation*

Americans tend to plan and implement quickly. This can lead to failure to produce a quality product. But failure is allowed in American companies since they feel that any problems or mistakes can be fixed as they arise.

■ *Concerned about efficiency*

Americans want to accomplish the job with a minimum expenditure of time and effort.

■ *Pragmatic about time*

The Japanese are flexible about time and believe in keeping everything in harmony. They tend to resist deadlines until they are sure they can meet them and are very meticulous about keeping appointments. Meetings don't tend to have deadlines but continue until all business has been completed. Taking time is seen as a sign of wisdom and sincerity. Upper level managers cannot be reached on short notice. A delay in keeping an appointment may be a polite way of saying they aren't interested.

■ *Long planning time but quick implementation*

The Japanese need to build consensus since it is important that everyone affected agree to the decision. This takes a long time. But once consensus is achieved, they quickly implement the agreed upon plan.

■ *Concerned about effectiveness*

The Japanese are concerned with results and consequences. As a result, it can take much longer to do things in Japan and much patience is necessary.

United States

■ *Communication tool*

Some meetings are brainstorming for ideas; some are to disseminate information; some are to discuss, defend and decide.

Americans like to get down to business right away since meetings are usually tightly scheduled and have a fixed agenda. A meeting may be adjourned before all business is completed. Americans also always like to leave with some kind of action plan.

Meetings can become very heated with a number of confrontations and disagreements to be resolved.

■ *Joking common*

Americans believe joking can relieve stress and keep relations informal and friendly. In formal business meetings or presentations, joking will be limited.

■ *Gather information*

Meetings are open to almost anyone since they are for the purpose of gathering information and not making decisions. Decisions are made only when there is complete consensus by everyone involved and this is done outside of the meeting. Meeting discussions will often be interrupted while the Japanese talk among themselves. Finally they will ask for time to think things over in order to start building the necessary consensus.

■ *Joking unacceptable*

Japanese take work seriously. Only after you prove you are good at work do you have the right to be silly and make jokes. They also seldom understand American jokes since jokes are based on an individual culture.

However, the Japanese do like to joke and have a good time after work.

United States

■ *Presentations*

Americans tend to have a projecting style of presentation. They often combine informative and persuasive styles as an efficient method of presentation. They attempt to persuade the audience to make a decision or take an action at the same time as they provide information. They consider this an effective and efficient use of time. Americans also believe in the "hard sell" and "quick close" approach to selling. They expect the audience to ask questions and to test the presenter's knowledge. Presenters expect to defend their opinions.

■ *Like detailed legal agreements*

Americans like to have all contingencies spelled out and believe an agreement is not binding until is it signed.

■ *Presentations*

The Japanese are non-projecting and restrained in speaking style and tend to use small gestures. They like to have the speaker's views presented clearly, logically and firmly.

They also like evidence of product quality and reliability included. The Japanese also appreciate visual images. The Japanese are basically non-argumentative and are uncomfortable with American attempts to be persuasive.

■ *Oral agreements common*

Japanese believe in oral agreements. Detailed American-style contracts make them suspicious. This indicates to them that trust has not been established. They like to emphasize flexibility, willingness to make adjustments, and pragmatism. Litigation means total loss of harmony.

United States

■ *Task oriented*

Americans are highly task oriented rather than relationship oriented. They are good at taking responsibility and pushing things through to a conclusion. They are more interested in the technical aspects of negotiation than in building relationships.

■ *Like agendas*

Presentations during negotiations are usually fairly formal and Americans like appeals to logic rather than emotion. They also like agendas for negotiation sessions and expect these agendas to be adhered to. They like fast-paced negotiations.

They also tend to attack issues sequentially, resolving them one issue at a time.

■ *Relationship oriented*

The major purpose of negotiations to the Japanese is to see if the two companies can get along over the long term. The Japanese want to build a personal relationship and this can take a long time. They will want to know your age, the university you attended, about your family and in general, about your background.

The Japanese prize quiet accommodation and emphasize personal obligations. Because negotiations are so dependent on personal relationships, negotiations, in a way, never end.

■ *Dislike agendas*

To the Japanese, negotiating is a form of conflict and they very strongly dislike conflict. Therefore, they do not like formal negotiations which implies agendas and a set of issues to be addressed.

The Japanese like to spend a lot of time asking very detailed questions in order to find out the position of the other company. They try to encompass this within their own position.

They also prefer informal negotiations in which time is spent building long-term relationships built on trust.

United States

■ *Highly detailed contracts*

Americans are very legalistic and like detailed contracts with all contingencies spelled out. These contracts tend to be fairly inflexible and are expected to be adhered to.

■ *Handling differences*

Americans are very open and direct in their communication. If there is a problem, they like to deal with it directly. They also tend to be rather poor listeners and have a tendency to interrupt.

Americans tend to see negotiations as adversarial with a win/lose attitude.

■ *Contracts less detailed*

To the Japanese, good intentions are more important than specific details in a contract. They also feel that signing a contract is not the end of negotiations. Negotiations are always on-going.

Contracts must be approved at each level of a company and this is very time consuming. The Japanese consensus-building, decision-making process is very complex.

The Japanese tend to focus on the long-term viability of a company rather than short-term profit or cash flow.

■ *Handling differences*

The Japanese are very non-confrontational. They like to avoid abrupt, direct statements or questions. They will not give a direct "no" to a proposal as this is considered very rude. Surface harmony is very important. It is also extremely important to never embarrass another person.

The Japanese can seem very rigid when dealing with differences due to their complex consensus-building process. They do not make a proposal until they feel completely comfortable with it and then they do not want to make concessions.

United States

■ *Present issues sequentially*

Americans tend to attack issues one at a time in sequence. They resolve one problem before moving on to the next.

■ *Summary*

Americans are often too impatient when negotiating, which can lead them to make unnecessary concessions.

Americans also tend to prefer to negotiate alone or in groups of less than five rather than in larger teams. This can become overwhelming especially if the other side has a team.

Americans generally have limited experience with other cultures. This can lead many American negotiators to become too concerned with the technical part of the negotiation and forget about building relationships with the other people.

■ *Present issues in groups*

The Japanese tend to consider issues in groups rather than one at a time. They need to see how all factors relate to and affect each other. This can be time consuming and requires patience from the other side.

They often ask a lot of detailed questions in order to find out the position of the other side and then encompass this into their own position.

■ *Summary*

The Japanese do not tend to be particularly strong at negotiating since they see it as a form of conflict. They dislike debate and if the other side becomes too aggressive they will simply withdraw.

They like to negotiate in large teams and dislike surprises. It is best to be very clear about your position with the Japanese and do not deviate very much.

If the Japanese truly like a proposal, they will say something like "We agree" and then elaborate. "Yes" does not mean agreement. If they say they will "seriously consider" a proposal, this means they need to consult with colleagues.

Many Japanese listen with closed eyes, and a smile means they are really listening.

U.S. Business Etiquette

- Be punctual. Americans are very time conscious. They also tend to conduct business at a fairly fast pace.

- A firm handshake and direct eye contact is the standard greeting.

- Direct eye contact is very important in business. Not making eye contact implies boredom or disinterest.

- Gift giving is not common. The United States has bribery laws which restrict the value of gifts which can be given.

- The United States is not particularly rank and status conscious. Titles are not used when addressing executives. Americans usually like to use first names very quickly. Informality tends to be equated with equality.

- Business meetings usually start with a formal agenda and tasks to be accomplished. There is usually very little small talk. Participants are expected to express their ideas openly; disagreements are common.

- If there is no one to introduce you at a business meeting, you may introduce yourself and present your card.

- Permission should be asked before smoking.

Japanese Business Etiquette

- **Very formal.** The Japanese always talk business except at the beginning of the first meeting. At that time they exchange business cards, drink tea and find out who you are, where you fit into the company's pecking order, and how your status relates to their status. Senior managers usually sit near windows; junior personnel are crowded in the center. Do not call a Japanese by his or her first name.

- **Signs of disapproval.** Hesitancy in speech, distressed facial expressions, unwillingness to be specific are signs that they do not like what you are saying. Temporary silence does not mean disapproval; they are probably just thinking over what you said.

- **Entertainment.** Eating is ritualistic, communal and time-consuming in Japanese business. The interaction is considered more important than the food. Avoid bringing your spouse to a business dinner. Your Japanese host usually will be male and will not bring his spouse. Japan is still male oriented and this is changing slowly. As of yet there are few women in professional positions. Real entertaining is done in the evening. Entertainment is lavish. Alcohol flows freely. This is the time Japanese usually say what they really think.

U.S. Gestures

■ Americans tend to stand an arms length away from each other.

■ Americans generally respect queues or lines. To shove or push one's way into a line will often result in anger and verbal complaint.

■ Beckoning is done by raising the index finger and curling it in and out, or by raising the hand and curling the fingers back toward the body.

■ Using the hand and index finger to point at objects or to point directions is common.

■ Whistling is a common way to get the attention of someone at a distance.

■ "No" is signalled by waving the forearm and hand (palm out) in front and across the upper body, back and forth.

■ Americans use the standard OK sign, the V for victory sign and the thumbs up sign.

- Formal introductions and ritual are very important.
- It is considered impolite to yawn in public.
- You should sit erect with both feet on the floor.
- Beckoning is done with palm down instead of up.
- Pointing is done with the whole hand.
- Shaking one hand from side to side with the palm forward means no.
- The Japanese often laugh when they are embarrassed.
- Avoid chewing gum in public
- Gift giving is common; try to give thoughtful and tasteful gifts.
- The Japanese are very polite and believe in humility.
- Address people by their title as well as name. Do not suggest using first names.
- When shaking hands, avoid being too firm or "pumping."
- The Japanese tend to display little facial emotion although they will smile a lot.
- Dress very conservatively and formally.

Communication Interferences

Effective communication, both verbal and nonverbal, means that the sending and processing of information between people, countries and businesses is understood, examined, interpreted, and responded to in some way. Any factor that causes a barrier or eliminates the successful transmission of information is defined as a communication interference.

- **Environmental interference** is an actual physical disturbance in the environment such as power outage, unregulated temperatures, a person or group talking very loud, etc.

- **Physiological interference** can be a hearing loss, laryngitis, illness, stuttering, neurological or organic deficit, etc.

- **Semantic interference**. We understand a word to have a certain meaning but the other person has a different meaning. Body language and gestures mean different things to different people. This includes confusion of abbreviated organizational jargon and pronunciation. Universal meanings (semantic understanding) are rare.

- **Syntactic interference**. Words are placed in certain order to give our language meaning. If the words are out of order, the meaning may be changed (this includes grammar).

- **Organizational interference.** Ideas being discussed lack sequence and can't be followed.

- **Psychological interference.** Words that incite emotion are used. In any emotional state (positive or negative) emotions need to be diffused in order to communicate effectively.

- **Social interference.** This includes cultural manners that are inappropriate for the country such as accepted codes for dress, business etiquette, communication rules, social activity.

Always become well informed about the customs and culture and get information before you try and do business in another country. Review this book and decide which areas of communication you and your colleagues will have difficulty with in Japan. Anticipate and plan accordingly.

As the visitor to another country, you need to move out of your "comfort zone." Make the people from another country feel comfortable doing business with you.

Succeeding in International Business

No one country has a lock on world markets. Fundamental changes have occurred in the world economy in the last decade. New technologies and low labor costs often give nations that once were not major players an advantage. This results in increased competition. Yet international business is vital to any country's prosperity.

Business is conducted by people and the future of any country in a global economy will lie with people who can effectively think and act across ethnic, cultural and language barriers. We need to understand that the differences between nations and cultures is profound. The European-based culture of the U.S. has very different values and behaviors than other cultures in the world. If you cannot accept and adapt to these differences, you will not succeed.

Companies striving to market their business overseas can become truly successful only when they recognize that the key is operating with sensitivity toward the culture of the other country. Communication cannot be separated from culture and this is true when doing business in other countries.

No flourishing company would present themselves to another company in their own country without researching that company's business culture and then adapting their image to meet the customer's comfort level.

It's the same when doing business in another country. You must adapt your image by using your knowledge of effective cultural communication to present a positive public image to the other country.

The first thing is to identify your target audience: clients, customers, suppliers, financial persons, government employees and so on. Then you must learn how to effectively communicate with them and this means learning the culture.

Business failure internationally rarely results from technical or professional incompetence. Americans tend to lack an understanding of what people from other countries want, how they work and so on. This lack of understanding can put a company at a tremendous disadvantage.

Learning the business protocol and practices of the country where you want to do business can give you great leverage. The more you know about the people you do business with, the more successful you can be. Businesspeople must make every contact they have with a foreign customer or business partner a positive one. Business leaders and managers must rethink the way they do business in the new global marketplace.

Succeeding in International Business

To be successful in the global market, you must:

- **Be flexible.** Cultural adaptations are necessary for individuals from both countries to get along and do business. Resisting the local culture will only lead to distrust.

- **Be patient.** Adjust your planning. Initiating business in many countries takes a long range approach and may require two or three years. Anticipate problems and develop alternative strategies.

- **Prepare thoroughly.** Research the country, the organization, the culture and beliefs of the people you will be dealing with.

- **Know your bottom line.** Know exactly what you want from a deal and at what point an agreement in not in your best interest. Know when to walk away.

- **Form relationships.** Encourage getting involved with the new community if you are going to be in the country for a long period.

- **Keep your cool.** Pay attention to the wide range of national cultural, religious and social differences you encounter.

- **Show respect.** Search for the other side's needs and interests. Accentuate the positive. Don't preach your own beliefs, and respect their beliefs.

When you are using this booklet, review your own beliefs and values about correct business protocol and ethics. Then match these ideas with the business practices and protocol in Japan.

You can contribute to your own success by recognizing that you will have to move out of your own "comfort zone" of doing business into the cultural business zone of Japan in order to develop the rapport necessary to meet the needs of your client or partner. This does not mean you compromise your company's image or product but that you do business following Japan's protocol while there. It's only for a short time that you may be following their rules and the payoff can be one in which concepts can be sold while still maintaining a consistent image and approach that is culturally appropriate.

- The United States is a very ethnically diverse country. To do business, it is important to be open to this diversity and to be flexible.

- Americans tend to be very individually oriented and concerned with their own careers. Their first loyalty is to themselves.

- Americans want to be liked. The prefer people who are good team players and want to cooperate.

- Americans value equality and dislike people who are too status or rank conscious.

- Most Americans are open, friendly, casual and informal in their manners. They like to call people by their first names quickly.

- Americans like to come right to the point and are uncomfortable with people who are indirect and subtle.

- Americans expect people to speak up and give their opinions freely and to be honest in the information they give. They like to have a direct and specific "yes" or "no."

- Americans can be very persistent. When they conclude a business transaction and sign a contract, they expect it to be honored. They do not like people who change their minds later.

- Write it down. While not good at spoken English, the Japanese are quite good at written English. You may also want to write down numbers.

- Avoid praise of your product or services. Let your literature or go-between discuss these subjects.

- Leave your lawyers and accountants home but bring a good interpreter.

- Learn at least a few words in their language.

- Look on your time in Japan as an educational experience; learn and participate in the culture.

- Japanese believe that good companies have the following formula for operating:
    - Good management techniques
    - Encouraging employees to come forward with ideas
    - Quarterly meetings so everyone knows how the business is doing
    - Total Quality Management that significantly reduces waste and improves the product

Be prepared to address these four issues with the Japanese according to how your company plans to do business with them.

Good morning	ohayo-gozaimasu (0-HAIo-o-zai-MAHSS)
Good afternoon	kon nichi wa (KON-nee-tshee-WAH)
Good evening	konban wa (KON-bahn-WAH)
My name is	watakushi wa ... desu (WAH-tah-kshee-WAH ... DEHSS)
What's your name?	onamae wa nan desu ka? (a-NAH-MAEH-WAH NAN dehss KAH)
Pleased to meet you	oai dekite koei desu (o-AI DEH-kteh KO-EHEE DEHSS)
Mr/Miss/Mrs	san (suffixed to name)
How are you?	ogenki desu ka? (o-GEHN-keedehss-KAH)
Fine, thank you	genki desu (GEHN-kee DEHSS)

Excuse me *(pardon me)*	sumimasen (SU-meemahsehn)
Excuse me *(I have to leave)*	shitsurei shimasu (SHEE-tsurey shee-MAHSS)
Excuse me *(sorry to bother you)*	gomen kudasai (GO-mehn kudah-SAI)
Thank you	arigato gozaimasu (ah-REE-ngah-TO-o go-zai-MAHSS)
Yes/No	hai/ile (HAI/EE-ee EH)
Good bye	sayonara

Notes

Available in this series:

Business China

Business France

Business Germany

Business Japan

Business Mexico

Business Taiwan

For more information, please contact:

Sales and Marketing Department
NTC Publishing Group
4255 West Touhy Avenue
Lincolnwood, IL 60646
708-679-5500